THE FUTURE OF WORK
What It Means for Individuals, Businesses, Markets and Governments

By David Bollier

THE ASPEN INSTITUTE

Communications and Society Program
Charles M. Firestone
Executive Director
Washington, D.C.
2011

To purchase additional copies of this report, please contact:

The Aspen Institute
Publications Office
P.O. Box 222
109 Houghton Lab Lane
Queenstown, Maryland 21658
Phone: (410) 820-5326
Fax: (410) 827-9174
E-mail: publications@aspeninstitute.org

For all other inquiries, please contact:

The Aspen Institute
Communications and Society Program
One Dupont Circle, NW
Suite 700
Washington, DC 20036
Phone: (202) 736-5818
Fax: (202) 467-0790

Charles M. Firestone   Patricia K. Kelly

Executive Director   *Assistant Director*

The Aspen Institute
One Dupont Circle, NW
Suite 700
Washington, DC 20036

Published in the United States of America in 2010
by The Aspen Institute

Printed in the United States of America

ISBN: 0-89843-543-9

11/004

Contents

Foreword

The speed by which information can now be shared—instantly and on a large horizontal scale—is causing tremors in many institutions that have enjoyed relative stability in the past. The "digital disruption" has come to industries, such as music and news, economies, such as the global financial markets, and even diplomacy and governance, as Wikileaks has shown.

The nature of work is no exception to this trend. Many people now earn their livings in an environment of constant connectivity and change. Mobile devices, social networks and cloud computing present new opportunities for individuals and organizations that are altering the DNA of the workplace and the worker.

People now have a multitude of jobs and career changes over the course of their working lives, different from the norm just a few decades ago. In the last year, the *New York Times* reports, the percentage of temporary workers hired in the private sector has skyrocketed, with many businesses now organizing "around short- to medium-term projects that can be doled out to temporary or contract workers."[1] It is unclear how the security and benefits of the traditional permanent job will be replaced. Firms utilize crowdsourcing to build innovations and markets, meaning they are able to slim down their employee base and simultaneously expand it by millions. Work and compensation are changing dramatically, with enormous implications for firms, the economy, governance and individual well-being.

There was no shortage of these matters to discuss when the Aspen Institute Roundtable on Information Technology met from August 3-6, 2010, to take on the "The Future of Work." Bringing together a diverse group of technologists, innovators, business leaders, entrepreneurs, academics and international politicians, the Roundtable's objective was to identify how long-term as well as quickly fomenting technological and social trends are changing the nature of work and firms, and also, importantly, to understand what comes next from it. Ultimately it sought to define a world of work that was not just more economically efficient but better for the people living in it.

---

1. Motoko Rich, "Weighing Costs, Companies Favor Temporary Help," *New York Times*, December 19, 2010, at http://www.nytimes.com/2010/12/20/business/economy/20temp.html

This report captures the themes and insights that arose over the three days, placing them in an understandable context and narrative, which rapporteur David Bollier is exceptionally adroit at doing.

In examining 21st century business realities such as decentralized workforces and firms leveraging communities and networks, the report captures the opportunities present for more rapid innovation, more efficient production and greater global reach. But questions arise about how workers gain skills and satisfaction from work, how they embrace change and how to govern the firm and society. When people are hyper-connected with no clear demarcation between work and home-life, how does the individual balance the two?

As work moves towards more open platforms, becoming less hier-archical, other aspects of society are also affected. The report explores how this changing force in the workplace poses the need for various institutional reforms to address increasing economic inequality, social marginalization, and systems of education and governance that are not keeping up with the changes. Or, as one participant asks, "What is the core competency of a government in a world where the old busi-ness model is not necessarily relevant any more?" How do employers, workers, educators and governments respond to the changing nature of work and the movement of firms to the virtual?

This report raises the right questions. The answers will no doubt change as rapidly as the technology does.

Acknowledgements

We thank our senior sponsor McKinsey & Company for its leadership in developing this Roundtable. In addition, we thank Google, Text100, John Rendon and John Kunzweiler for sponsoring this conference; James Manyika, Bill Coleman, Hal Varian and Gilman Louie for helping to organize the program, and Michael Chui for aiding in suggesting participants and readings. Most especially, we thank each of the participants, listed in the Appendix, for their valuable input at the Roundtable. Finally, we thank Peter Keefer, Project Manager, and Tricia Kelly, Assistant Director of the Communications and Society Program, for their extensive efforts in producing this report and the Roundtable itself.

Charles M. Firestone
Executive Director
Communications and Society Program
Washington, D.C.
February 2011

THE FUTURE OF WORK

WHAT IT MEANS FOR INDIVIDUALS, BUSINESSES, MARKETS AND GOVERNMENTS

David Bollier

THE FUTURE OF WORK

What It Means for Individuals, Businesses, Markets and Governments

By David Bollier

Introduction

Over the course of the past generation, but especially since the World Wide Web emerged in 1994, digital technologies have been transforming the nature of work, the architectures of markets and the inner dynamics of organizations. They have also been altering the global economy and national cultures, which in turn is forcing governments to change how they build infrastructure, meet social needs and provide services.

Historically, the pace of change has been fairly incremental, which has partially masked the depth of transformation underway. In recent years, however, the metabolism of change has accelerated. Novel media platforms and new efficiencies introduced by a convergence of technologies—computing, telecommunications, wireless systems, mobile devices and more—are sending shockwaves across society. The worlds of work, the marketplace, organizations of all sorts, personal life and global commerce are being transformed as systems from Facebook to Twitter and smart phones to e-readers give rise to a strange new social-economic-political ecosystem.

Some things are clear. The networked environment is rapidly changing employment relationships while offering new opportunities for boosting productivity and competing more effectively. It is also disrupting centralized organizations and fueling the rise of flexible work teams and dynamic, niche markets. It is less clear how employers, individual workers and governments should respond to these changes, or how these changes will play out over the long term. Any map of the emerging landscape still has numerous blank spots bearing the warning, "Here be dragons!"

1

To explore this rich territory and try to develop a better map of its topography, the Aspen Institute Communications and Society Program convened a three-day conference, "The Future of Work," August 4–6, 2010. The event brought together 23 technologists, entrepreneurs, venture capitalists, computer industry experts, management consultants, workforce specialists and academics to try to make sense of the changes now transforming work in its many dimensions. The discussions were moderated by Charles M. Firestone, Executive Director of the Communications and Society Program. This report is an interpretive synthesis of those discussions and the key themes raised.

We start in Part I with an overview of how 20th century business models—based on large standardization and mass production to maximize efficiency and profit—are giving way to a new breed of business models that seek to leverage the power of digital networking.

As we will see in Part II, this new context for businesses—a world of ubiquitous Internet access, capacious bandwidth and memory storage, and rapidly evolving software and devices—is dramatically changing the organization of work and empowering workers. Despite the uncertainties and risks, enterprises that embrace open platforms and relationship-driven business strategies are discovering new competitive advantages.

Leveraging the new business models, however, requires that the "worker of tomorrow" be able to cultivate certain dispositions and skill sets that are not necessarily prized in conventional work environments. These themes are explored in Part III. The firm of the future will be different, too. Business leaders, therefore, need to understand the competitive strategies and organizational norms that will succeed in the networked environment—the focus of Part IV.

The repercussions of digital networks go beyond the marketplace. They implicate government and public policy in significant ways. The question is whether and how governments, educational institutions and other social institutions will address the formidable challenges that lie ahead. These questions are explored in Part V.

It remains an open question what sorts of institutional and policy reforms may be needed to address the disruptive, antisocial aspects of the new marketplace: economic inequality, social marginalization, deficient educational opportunities. Governments and schools at all levels are only beginning to explore how they may need to change to help individuals, firms and social institutions thrive in the new environment.

Any assessment of these issues is necessarily fraught with uncertainties, disagreement and sheer speculation. That said, the participants of this roundtable identified many powerful trends—some hopeful, others alarming—that will surely intensify in coming years.

I. The 21st Century Workplace

A good place to start this exploration of the future of work is by reviewing the past: the familiar 20th century patterns of employment, education, training and career advancement. These models continue to guide our thinking, even as they begin to crumble in the face of new 21st century realities.

In his 2001 book, *The Future of Success*, former U.S. Labor Secretary Robert Reich writes that the idea of the steady, permanent job is becoming a relic of another era, or more precisely, the postwar period of American life.[1] During this period, he notes, people implicitly expected that a job would consist of "steady work with predictably rising pay," especially if they were loyal to the company and accrued seniority at the firm.

Employees in the second half of the 20th century were generally paid more for their "clock time" at work than for specific outcomes, in part because most individual employees had strictly prescribed responsibilities. Most jobs were designed as "mechanical" cogs in a larger production apparatus whose purpose was to maximize economies of scale. "The organization ran by rules," writes Reich. "Factory workers were not paid to think. Henry Ford once complained that when he hired a pair of hands, he also got a human being. Where no rules were available, there were rules for setting new rules. If the vast organizational machine was to attain maximum efficiency, all behavior had to be fully anticipated."[2]

Michael Chui, Senior Fellow at the McKinsey Global Institute of the McKinsey & Company consulting firm, offered a short presentation contrasting the "Sloan Age" of organizational management—a shorthand for workplace design in the 20th century—with emerging trends in work structures and practices (Alfred P. Sloan was the legend-ary Chairman of General Motors from 1937 to 1956 who introduced extensive "scientific management" techniques in organizing automo-bile production).

Chui summarized the conventional wisdom about organizing work in the 20th century this way:

> The best way to harness human talent is through full-time, exclusive employment relationships where people are paid for the amount of time they spend at a common location. They should be organized in stable hierarchies where they are evalu-ated primarily through the judgment of their superiors, and what and how they do their jobs is prescribed.

Chui proceeded to isolate key phrases from this summary in order to show the contrast between old norms and emerging trends:

"Full-time, exclusive employment relationship." Work tasks are increasingly being accomplished through "crowdsourcing" techniques, in which software platforms enable Internet users to contribute to a project without necessarily getting paid.

"Paid for the amount of time [spent at work]." Companies are increas-ingly hosting contests as a way to elicit new ideas and tap into com-munity knowledge, noted Chui. For example, in 2006, Netflix offered a prize of $1 million to anyone who could increase the accuracy of its movie recommendation system by 10 percent. The company offered a data set of over 100 million movie ratings from more than 480,000 users rating 18,000 movies, and they received numerous useful sugges-tions that offered "sub-10 percent improvements" before finally award-ing $1 million in equity in September 2009.

The toymaker Lego took a similar approach with its Lego CAD [computer-aided design] package, a toy that both children and adults use to design their own Lego systems. By hosting a website called the Lego Digital Designer, Lego received many toy designs that they pro-ceeded to re-package and sell. The site leverages the community of customers to obtain free research and development.

"Common location." The idea of a workplace as a fixed, physi-cal location is changing as work becomes more distributed through technology, said Chui. So, for example, some companies use "near-shoring"—the outsourcing of work to people working at home in the

U.S. —while other organizations are "born global" as virtual enterprises that electronically link management, designers, manufacturing, marketing and other tasks.

"Stable hierarchies." The flattening of corporate hierarchies is now quite familiar, but some companies are going much further, using social-networking technologies to staff their projects, said Chui. Instead of specific jobs, some companies are modularizing their work into discrete projects and sourcing them not just with current employees but with former ones as well. Still other companies are using online markets to identify talent, make predictions about the future and generate new ideas and knowledge.

"Evaluated primarily through the judgment of their superiors." Instead of a single boss or management team evaluating the performance of an employee, alternative means of appraising performance are emerging. Chui described a "720-degree evaluation"—a twist on the "360-degree evaluation" in which everyone within a company evaluates an employee. In a 720-degree evaluation, people *outside* of the organization also evaluate the employee. A person's *degree of connectedness* and *influence in a network* is also evaluated. Finally, some employees are evaluated based on their "trading ability" on online prediction markets.

"What and how they do their jobs is prescribed." A new management mindset is needed in the "post-Sloan Age" environment, said Chui. In the 20th century, managers focused on standardized procedures, patterns of interaction among employees, the work plan and predicted outcomes. But in the new environment, managers must focus on how employees participate in informal communities of work or practice. Following fixed work plans is seen as less valuable than the ability to experiment and follow up. "You don't know ahead of time what's going to work," said Chui, "so you have to follow the successes and figure out how to make them really powerful and scale them." The central role of technology, then, might not be enforcing compliance, but enabling participation.

For business analysts John Hagel III, John Seely Brown and Lang Davison, work in the 20th century embodied a "push" worldview—an approach to business organization that is based on forecasting market demand and then "pushing" out production outputs to customers.[3] As the authors write in their 2010 book, *The Power of Pull*, "Push works mightily to ensure that the right people and resources are delivered at the right place and the right time to serve the anticipated demand."

Under "push" systems, companies build up inventory in advance of demand. They develop standard routines that use "tightly scripted specifications of activities designed to be invoked by known parties in predetermined contexts." Push strategies are exemplified by thick process manuals, regimented manufacturing and service models, schools that teach the same curricula to everyone, and television networks that adhere to programming formulas guided by fixed demographic metrics and ratings.

The scientific management of work as pioneered by Frederick Taylor is a classic "push" approach. It is a top-down administered regime that seeks to control activities in great detail in order to maximize predictable outcomes. It seeks efficiency and uniformity throughout the system. Not surprisingly, workers and consumers alike are regarded as passive vessels who must conform to the needs of system; most workers are now allowed to express their own human agency beyond narrow limits.

The philosophy of "push," write Hagel, Brown and Davison, requires small groups of elites and experts to direct an enterprise's operations and allocate resources. In turn, this requires a centralized hierarchy committed to command and control of an apparatus of mass production and consumption. The firm of the 20th century, write Hagel et al., "was built on the premise that the primary role of the firm was to arrive at lower costs by getting bigger—to make the most of the scale economies available through the new infrastructures of the day [electricity, railroads, airfreight, containerized shipping], what we call 'scalable efficiency'."[4]

The rise and proliferation of computers, the Internet and other digital technologies are shattering many of the core premises of 20th century firms and markets. In the turbulent new world of ubiquitous networks and digital technologies, Taylorite schemes of work and business organization tend to be less effective, moot or counterproductive.

We will examine some of these tensions between the old and new in coming sections, but first, it is useful to pause and reflect on the very definitions of "work" and "workplace." What were once fairly stable, self-evident terms are themselves becoming more fluid, blurry and postmodern.

What Is "Work"?

It is not self-evident how to define "work," given that work is not just an artifact of the marketplace, but equally a personal and social phenomenon. For Robert Morris, Vice President of Services Research for IBM Research, it is useful to apply systems analysis to define work. Work can be seen as "human activity" bounded only by the amount of waking time in a day (with a concession that sleep may help organize productive thought).

"It's a beautiful, gigantic *system*—a 'stock-and-flow' model—that produces goods, services, fun and happiness," said Morris. "It's a systems model of peoples' time and behavior as an input together with positive and negative feedback in the form of incentives that determine the productivity and quality of the outputs."

For most workers in the 20th century, it is fair to say that there was a clear demarcation between "work" and "home" and between "work" and "play." One's identity and focus at work—in producing some measurable unit of market value for a manufacturer, service provider or government—was quite separate from one's identity and focus at home.

No more. "Work" is no longer confined to a specific time and place. As if to reinvent the lost world of artisanal tradition, technology is blurring the lines between work and home and between work and personal life. Tens of millions of people now work at home offices, telecommute or participate in "virtual companies" whose members are scattered across the country or the globe. Many others work for startup firms in improvised settings.

"Work in the future will be organized in ways that are far more decentralized," said Thomas W. Malone, Director of the MIT Center for Collective Intelligence. "I think we are in the early stages of an increase in human freedom in business that may, in the long run, be as important a change for business as the change to democracy was for governments. This is happening because cheap communication lets more people have enough information that they can make sensible decisions for themselves instead of just following orders from people above them in the hierarchy. And that means

> **"Work in the future will be organized in ways that are far more decentralized."**
>
> *Thomas Malone*

we can have the economic benefits of large-scale enterprises, such as efficiency and scale, and at the same time have the human benefits of small scale, such as motivation, creativity and flexibility."

The workplace of the 21st century may not even *be* a workplace, noted Dwayne Spradlin, President and CEO of InnoCentive, Inc., a virtual business that offers an "open innovation" platform for the crowdsourcing of solutions. Work is no longer an activity that occurs at a particular *place*, nor is it even an activity confined to a distinct period of *time.*

Work is also moving beyond familiar cognitive definitions, said John Seely Brown, Independent Co-Chairman of the Deloitte Center for the Edge. "We've got to recognize that the real high-value work, ironically, may not fit within our classical cognitive framework, but may actually have an *imaginative* component. A tremendous amount of my work is done in my sleep. That is to say, there are parts of imaginative think-ing that are definitely not conscious, but probably subconscious, that require 'lateral connections' that are not necessarily cognitive."

"Beyond cognitive competencies," said Maryam Alavi, Vice Dean of the Goizueta Business School at Emory University and holder of the John and Lucy Cook Chair of Information Strategy, "there is a whole arena of emotional intelligence. This involves knowing one's self, being able to self-manage, being able to connect to others and being able to show empathy toward others. There are also competencies around social relations that relate to teamwork, negotiation and conflict man-agement. And then there are behavioral competencies that involve our actions." In short, the work of the future may require much more "holistic thinking."

"The most effective individuals," Alavi continued, "are those who have a well-rounded development of these sets of skills, and they know which one to apply. In fact, there are some newer studies of brain imag-ing that show that very effective strategic thinkers fire on various parts of the brain related to these different sets of competencies."

Does a person's motivation matter in how we define "work"? Is the fact that someone is paying for work what makes it "work"? Kim Taipale, Founder and Executive Director of the Stilwell Center for Advanced Studies in Science and Technology Policy, said, "When my gardener weeds, it's work, but when I weed, it's sort of what I do."

Work seems to involve activity that is being done *at someone else's behest*. It is something that has to be done whether or not you enjoy doing it. Or as Shami Khorana, President of HCL America, Inc., put it, "Work is working with people to bring value to some entity."

The globalization of work has made it more complicated to define what work is, said Tammy Johns, Senior Vice President for Innovation and Workforce Solutions at Manpower, Inc. Work responsibilities are becoming more complex and specialized, the boundaries between work and personal life are blurring, and the shift from manufacturing to services is putting a greater premium on people's ability to solve complex problems and show sophisticated judgment. Job responsibilities call for a richer, more subtle array of human talents.

With the profusion of such work, many people's jobs are coming to reflect their way of life. Personal and social motivations are very important to many entrepreneurs, for example, and also to many "free agents." "Right now I'm tracking about 50 virtual work marketplaces where work is being done on the Internet as either task-based work or projects," said Tammy Johns. "And what you see in those marketplaces is people working for the love of it. You also see people working to maintain a certain lifestyle." She added that a large number of these workers are "women and students who can work in these marketplaces from anywhere because it suits their lifestyle."

For much of the world, of course, work or its particular appeal is hardly an elective choice. It is a physical and personal necessity. Work is essential to eating and living. In India, for example, some 70 percent of the population is still dependent on agriculture, noted S. Gopalakrishnan, CEO and Managing Director of Infosys Technologies Ltd. Physical labor still predominates over the mental or "symbolic work" done via computers or offices.

The Coming Crisis in Organizing Work

In considering the future of work, roundtable participants shared a broad consensus that there is an unacknowledged crisis brewing. The fears were diverse: that individuals will not have the necessary skills to obtain paying work; that organizations will have trouble adapting to the networked environment and global competition; and that governments will not have the foresight, sophistication or courage to craft new types of public policies and governance structures.

Although participants agreed that information and communications technologies will yield many economic and social benefits, they worry about a future with greater economic inequality, social polarization, spasms of nationalism and protectionism, and international instability.

"We've got organizations that need to figure out how to make talent and work pools function globally," said Dwayne Spradlin of InnoCentive, Inc. "Organizations need to figure out a way to move from fixed procedures and infrastructure to variable ones in organizing and optimizing resources. And now we've got the millennial generation coming in, and if anything, they're more project-based, not jobs-based, which means we need to think about how to orchestrate work talent in an environment of constant churn. There is a need for a whole new business science that can help organizations function more effectively in this 'new normal,' if you will."

> **"There is a need for a whole new business science that can help organizations function more effectively in this 'new normal.'"**
>
> *Dwayne Spradlin*

Spradlin continued: "My sense is that there is a constant move toward globalization, outsourcing and the 'free-agent nation.' People are engaging the workplace in a very different way. I think over the next five years we're going to see a massive shift in demographics among young people and how they engage their organizations. In general, companies are wholly unprepared for what's about to come."

Robert Morris of IBM Research agreed that an "extreme state of crisis" is gathering, one that is driven by many factors. He cited a growing "bifurcation" of the workforce—those who are benefiting from economic development and those who are not. This trend is not only occurring within countries, but among them, he said. "A few billion people on the planet don't even get a K–12 education." The lack of education and opportunity is not only hurting the most impoverished people of the world, skill shortages can prevent companies and investors from growing their business and expanding the economy.

All of these trends are intensified by the velocity of change that tech-nology is driving. Paul Inouye, Partner at Perella Weinberg Partners, noted that the major trends of computing—mainframes in the '60s, PCs and client-servers in the '80s and the web in the late '90s—were once crashing upon society at a pace that might now be considered leisurely. Today, the growth of mobile communications, cloud com-puting, open software platforms and other major arenas of innovation are "condensing," he said. "Things are moving *very* quickly." Moreover, Inouye noted, what used to be a U.S.-centric phenomenon has become a large, international trend.

As the technological convergence proceeds, the dynamics of the com-munications/computing/social ecosystem are becoming more bewilder-ing and complex. Competition, cooperation and conflict can take place simultaneously among the same companies in a given market. People across the world are being knit together into virtual spaces, said Inouye, resulting in "this weird, dynamic collaboration in which you're physi-cally not even near the person you're actively collaborating with."

Yet with the focus so much on external customers, said Shami Khorana, workers organized to function in discrete work "silos" often find that they cannot coordinate and collaborate adequately with other workers in their own companies, "There is little focus on what their internal customers are saying, and how they should respond."

Any discussion of the future of work means "coming to grips with the problems of the world economy, world governments and business models," said Tim H. El-Hady, Director of Business Planning and Operations for Microsoft U.K. Ltd. "It means developing a vision."

El-Hady commended the Confucian philosophy in China and other religious philosophies that see the interests of society as overriding those of individuals and that honor the spirit of service to others. "The world is just so diversified, and only in the past 50 or 60 years have we been able to recognize our global connectedness, to view our wonderful planet with one eye, with a global perspective." El-Hady suggested that any new vision for the future of work must strive to integrate diverse human concerns into a coherent philosophical system that can recon-cile divergent values as efficiency, equality and justice.

As these comments suggest, discussions about the future of work can take place at many levels—world historical trends, ethical philosophy, global and domestic politics, economics, public policy, business strategy, and education policy, among other fields. All are implicated. But Dwayne Spradlin spoke for many conference participants when he accented the practical implications of failing to address the future of work: "If firms don't visualize what their futures look like and begin to make the changes that are necessary, those firms may cease to exist as we know them. We need a vision of what these firms should look like and how to transform our existing organizations."

II. How Technology is Changing Work

Jacques Bughin, Director of the Brussels Office of McKinsey & Company, argues—with co-authors James Manyika and Roger Roberts—that information technology is calling into question many time-honored premises about work, management and the corporation itself: "New degrees of freedom can be discovered in where and how companies compete, in how value is created, and in the nature of the corporation and how it is managed. Companies that exploit these new degrees of freedom can change the competitive game in their favor."

The authors make this case in an article, "New Degrees of Management Freedom: Challenging Sloan Age Business Orthodoxies," which appeared in the *McKinsey Technology Initiative Perspective*. [5] They continue:

> Transaction costs have tumbled in this wired world, and nearly ubiquitous connectivity has made new and unexpected ties with customers, talent and suppliers not only possible, but also easy. Digitization has changed the economics of creating and distributing products, services and content across a growing number of categories. It has the potential to revolutionize business, managerial and organizational models.

Bughin et al. provide a table of 10 business orthodoxies that are now being supplanted by "new freedoms" enabled by information technologies:

Orthodoxies		New Freedoms
1. Roles of companies and customers are distinct	→	Partners in co-creation
2. Competitive advantage from owning assets	→	Open assets—orchestration
3. Businesses start from traditional markets	→	Born global and blowback
4. Paying for value and talent	→	Value for free
5. Seek blockbusters	→	Mining the tail
6. Goods wear out	→	Goods improve with use
7. Power of bigness	→	Radical empowerment
8. Full-time employees in hierarchies	→	Everyone an employee
9. Batch	→	Real-time business
10. Trust your gut	→	Management science

One of the most intriguing "new freedoms" that networking technologies afford is item 4, the ability to generate value more efficiently, using "free" resources. "The Net allows the creation of 'multisided' markets, where one of the 'sides' can be free, and the other very profitable," write Bughin et al. "On the web, however, distribution costs are close to free, and the market is vast, creating adjacent profit pools that can be large. Web content sites from news sites to blog and photo sharing sites are prime examples of companies exploiting this freedom. These sites provide services for free in one market, e.g., for content, and then monetize their usage in another market, such as through advertising or by providing premium services...."

Other "new freedoms" are familiar but of growing importance. The Long Tail, for example, is the idea that that Internet can help bundle small, disaggregated consumer demand into viable niche markets, displacing the pressure to make "blockbuster" products that appeal to large, undifferentiated masses of consumers. The idea of consumers acting as co-creators with companies—as illustrated in the Lego and Netflix examples above—is also gaining momentum among many web-oriented businesses.

Important caveats were made, however: much of the world's work, especially hard, physical labor in Asia, Africa and other developing regions, is not likely to be affected by these trends in the near future, if ever. Even in India, only two million workers are in information technology businesses in a nation of one billion people, and many IT systems are not likely to transform many existing enterprises and types of labor. And yet, as the proliferation of mobile phones in the developing world has shown, the tech revolution is not confined to advanced capitalist economies. Furthermore, said Chui, there are already "weak signs" that post-Sloan Age dynamics are reaching many improbable business sectors and countries.

Crowdsourcing as a New Template for Work

The distributed outsourcing of work through an "open call" to any web user—a technique often called "crowdsourcing"—has become popular in many quarters as a way to reap smart, innovative research results quickly and efficiently.

One of the first major crowdsourcing projects, in 2005, was Amazon.com's Mechanical Turk, a Web 2.0 platform that enabled the creation of specific "Human Intelligence Tasks," or HITs, which self-selected people could carry out and get paid for.[6] "Crowdsourcing" now applies to many sorts of mass collaborations or competitions. It includes contests that gives prizes for the best, most innovative solutions to problems; open invitations to mass participation in solving design and software challenges; and distributed volunteer projects such as Distributed Proofreaders (to proofread public-domain texts) and the NASA Clickworkers Project (to classify craters on Mars).[7]

Crowdsourcing has become a full-fledged business model for some companies.

More than a technique for mass collaboration, crowdsourcing has become a full-fledged business model for some companies. InnoCentive, Inc. may be one of the most successful such enterprises. Based in Waltham, Massachusetts, the company acts as a broker between "seekers" with research and development problems and "solvers," who propose solutions that meet the desired criteria. Seekers are frequently large corporations with vexing challenges in engineering, computer science, chemistry and many other scientific fields. Solvers win cash awards for their efforts.

InnoCentive was started as a wholly owned subsidiary of Eli Lilly, the pharmaceutical maker, in 2001, when it realized that the cost of innovation in drug development was increasing faster than the revenue. The idea of distributed, open innovation seemed like a compelling idea worth exploring. InnoCentive is a virtual firm whose employees work from locations around the world using remote-networking technologies.

Dwayne Spradlin, President and CEO of InnoCentive, noted that knowledge-management systems of the 1980s and 1990s were "a complete and utter failure" because they focused on indexing and "pushing out" knowledge. InnoCentive seeks to mobilize "vast pools of productivity and intellectual capacity" in a very different way, through open platforms and mass participation. "We define a goal in a concrete way and then try to get people galvanized around that," said Spradlin.

"None of our crowdsourcing is about a free ride for business organizations," he added. "This is about getting the right people to work on the right problems at the right time. Why? Because our systems are failing." Recent InnoCentive projects—from among hundreds listed on its website—include "challenges" that invite freelance researchers to develop a cost-effective system to clean water in Sub-Saharan Africa, to propose ways to build a novel technology platform for the analysis of cellular metabolites, and to find efficient ways to discover freely available and openly accessible learning resources.

The work culture that Spradlin as CEO has cultivated at InnoCentive exemplifies many of the principles of the post-Sloan Age environment. It is a paragon of openness, with all financial numbers except core revenues and costs available for anyone to see. Employees are not required to sign nondisclosure agreements or noncompete contracts.

Employees are expected to be highly conversant with digital networking and virtual collaboration. And they are also expected to be passionate about their jobs. "It doesn't matter if you answer the phones or if you're a Ph.D.," said Spradlin, "you better be passionate about what we do. It's a calling. As a result, we have no turnover, absolutely no turnover."

He noted that InnoCentive also evaluates its employees on "outcome-based measures" that assess the impact they are having on the company's markets. Employees are also judged for their "relationship management skills" and their leadership. "Thirty percent of my team's bonuses and variable compensation is based upon leadership," Spradlin said. Since 2006, InnoCentive has expanded its services to a variety of new industry sectors, and its annual revenue growth has typically been between 50 and 80 percent.[8]

A notable feature of InnoCentive, observed Thomas Malone of the MIT Center for Collective Intelligence, is the fact that "hundreds of thousands of people all over the world are doing the core work of the company—that is, coming up with innovative ideas." This is a future trend, to be sure, said Bill Coleman, the serial software entrepreneur and Partner in Alsop Louie Partners. "The world is turning into a guild, so you can leverage all sorts of open-source collectives without having to do any of the drudge work to build platforms, systems and tools that you need."

The grand hope, of course, is that participatory technologies will enhance productivity among workers, especially among the highest level of "knowledge workers," whose work involves critical thinking, sophisticated judgment and problem solving. Machines can already do most of the work of bank tellers and supermarket-checkout clerks. But can we improve the productivity of a salesperson, healthcare worker, general manager or university professor, asked Michael Chui, Senior Fellow at the McKinsey Global Institute. "I think we are very early in this S-curve," he said, "and nowhere near the inflection point."

> ...technology can function as "reflective amplifiers" to enhance an individual worker's performance.
>
> *John Seely Brown*

Still, John Seely Brown of the Deloitte Center for the Edge believes that technology can function as "reflective amplifiers" to enhance an individual worker's performance. He cited the on-screen "dashboards" used by players of the online game "World of Warcraft" to assess their performance. "What would happen if employees could crate their own 'dashboards,' not for management, but to examine their own performance, how they're spending their time, and so on?" Brown asked. Such IT-assisted feedback loops could prove highly motivational and assist employees to continuously learn and modify their behaviors.

As cloud computing becomes more pervasive, Peter Jackson, Chief Scientist and Vice President of Corporate Research and Development at Thomson Reuters, envisions a similar improvement in employee performance. "Once the cloud becomes a reality and people have raw, undifferentiated computing power available to them as a utility, they will be able to stop worrying about infrastructure and platforms," said Jackson. "Then they will be able to start thinking about intangibles: innovation and imagination—the things that build higher quality services. I think this will raise everybody's game."

The Future of the Firm and the Importance of Size

The rise of crowdsourcing and other networking techniques raises a provocative question: Is the venerable "theory of the firm," as propounded by economist Ronald Coase in his famous 1937 essay, obsolete?

Coase's celebrated "transaction cost" theory of the firm stated that the economic rationale for forming a business enterprise is its ability to manage employees and production more efficiently than by contracting these functions out to the marketplace. A firm can minimize transaction costs, which are otherwise higher if one must buy those goods and services in the marketplace.

But now, if online markets can radically reduce transaction costs, over and above what a firm can achieve, is the economic justification for the business firm disappearing? Does the firm still need to exist?

Maryam Alavi, Vice Dean of the Goizueta Business School, thinks the answer is that organizational forms are going to become a lot more complex *internally* in order to respond to the increasing *external* complexity of the business environment. "This is based on the 'law of requisite variety' in systems theory. There are parts of the organization that are going to be more hierarchical because of the uncertainties that they deal with or don't deal with. And there are parts of the organization that will need to be highly dynamic, open and changing."

"So managing that complexity and form is going to be very important to organizations in the future," said Alavi. "And that's why quality of leadership is going to be increasingly important to organizations. It's important to realize that hierarchy and openness is not an either/or thing. It's a both/and kind of thing."

As a corollary to Alavi's insight, Kim Taipale, Founder and Executive Director of the Stilwell Center for Advanced Studies in Science and Technology Policy, cited Bateson's Rule, which holds (among other things) that "the only source of new patterns or new learning is *noise*." An organizational structure or hierarchy naturally attempts to suppress the noise of the network, in order to amplify the meaningful information, or signal. "But you can't take out all of the noise," said Taipale, "because then the network will never be resilient enough to deal with the shocks from the outside. So we have to find some way to balance noise and signal."

An analysis based on "transaction costs" may be missing the point. Perhaps the more meaningful axis for organizing firms today is their ability to intelligently filter "noise" from the network. Firms and employees must learn to balance noise and learning, so that they can respond appropriately, flexibly and rapidly to the complex and changing market environment.

If the boundaries of the firm are becoming more permeable and elastic, and if the internal structures of firms are themselves undergoing great change, does the size of firms matter? Will small firms have strategic advantages over large firms?

People no longer need to work through organizational hierarchies to do important work.

Thomas W. Malone

In a 1987 paper, Thomas W. Malone of MIT, working with co-authors JoAnne Yates and Robert I. Benjamin, concluded that information technology, by reducing the costs of coordination, would lead to an overall shift toward proportionately greater use of markets—rather than hierarchies—to coordinate economic activity. They predicted that the new efficiencies in coordination would result in "fundamental changes in how firms and markets organize the flow of goods and services."[9]

Drawing upon his 2004 book, *The Future of Work*,[10] Malone, speaking at the Aspen conference, suggested a different calculus for contemplating the future of the firm. Instead of asking, Where shall the organizational boundaries of the firm be drawn, Malone suggested we should be asking, What is the future of big and small decision making? People no longer need to work through organizational hierarchies to do important work. Because they are connected electronically, they can undertake "small activities" on their own, without authorization, and still have significant, often global impact.

The sheer proliferation of "small activities" occurring on digital networks, however, is generating some formidable challenges. Legacy hierarchies and elite managers continue to act as bottlenecks. This creates an insane crush of responsibilities for gatekeepers and decision makers. Not only is the flow of useful information and innovation inhibited, decision makers are being personally overwhelmed.

This phenomenon prompted Michael Chui to pose a disturbing question, What happens when external demands for connectivity exceed human capabilities to cope?

Chui cited a comment made by Eric Schmidt, the Chairman and CEO of Google, during an interview published by McKinsey Quarterly in September 2008: "For senior executives, it's probably the case that [life] balance is no longer possible. I would love to have balance in my life except that the world is a global stage and, when I'm sleeping, there's a crisis in some country, and I still haven't figured out how not to sleep. So the fact is that you're going to select executives who like the rush of the intensity. They're going to be drawn to the sense of a crisis. The sense of speed. And they are the ones, ultimately, who are going to rise to the top."

And the more balanced, well-rounded CEOs? As one CEO of a global corporation put it, "Pretty soon it'll get to the point where being the CEO of a major public company is no longer a desirable job."

The problem with these laments, said Thomas Malone, is that they presume the need for organizational hierarchies. "If you assume that there has to be a hierarchy and somebody has to be at the top of it, and that organizations will get bigger and bigger, and the connectivity will get greater and greater, then you're bound to reach a point where no human can really cope with it all. And the few that come close will not even want to."

So maybe we need to reframe the question, said Malone. Perhaps we should ask, "How can we redesign our organizations so that the demands for external connectivity do not exceed human abilities to cope?"

The standard response is to flatten and decentralize an organization, so that knowledge and decision making become more decentralized. In tackling this challenge, Kim Taipale suggested that perhaps we should shift the framework of discussion about value-creation from *firms* to *platforms.* The future may belong less to firms organized as hierarchies than to participants in open, networked platforms. Perhaps the most salient issue in generating value these days is not transaction costs, but *interaction costs*, said Taipale, because easy, efficient interaction among multiple participants on a network is the most powerful engine for innovation today.

> **The future may belong less to firms organized as hierarchies than to participants in open, networked platforms.**
>
> *Kim Taipale*

To put this in historical perspective, software entrepreneur Bill Coleman noted that the most powerful inflection points in the history of mankind have come when new tools were developed to leverage and expand collective intelligence. "The first instance was the development of language, and the second was the invention of the printing press. The third major inflection point is the rise of the Internet, said Coleman, because it represents two inflection points at once: "the quantity of communication and the speed of knowledge-creation and -formation."

III. The Workers of Tomorrow

What will the future of work mean for workers? S. Gopalakrishnan, CEO and Managing Director of Infosys Technologies Ltd., enumerated a list of skills and personal attributes that successful workers will need to succeed in the networked environment.

Every worker will have to become a continuous learner, he said, and will likely hold multiple jobs over the course of his or her lifetime, if not multiple careers. Many workers will need to work at part-time jobs and perhaps hold down multiple jobs simultaneously, he added. The ability to multitask and deal with interruptions to work will become mandatory skills.

Because work will become more modularized, workers will need to be specialized in certain skills—while still being able to communicate with the rest of a team. Many projects will be performed as "swarm work," in which "everybody jumps in and tries to solve the problem," Gopalakrishnan said. "This is becoming a viable model for certain types of work."

A great deal of existing work will be automated, he noted, but a great deal of work is likely to become less routine and more exception-based, especially in knowledge-based jobs. That said, even familiar jobs will begin to use information systems and become more knowledge intensive. "Many fishermen in India actually use their cell phones before coming ashore to find out which markets will offer the best prices for their fish," said Gopalakrishnan. "And the knowledge content for a bus driver today is very different from a bus driver of 30 or 40 years ago, because of the technology of the bus itself."

> **Many projects will be performed as 'swarm work,' in which "everybody jumps in and tries to solve the problem."**
>
> *S. Gopalakrishnan*

A great deal of useful product and service information can be gleaned from customers, using various sorts of electronic feedback. This advance will spur the development of new systems to actively solicit the views of customers as well as those of business partners and employees. "Today," said Gopalakrishnan, "We bring 10 people into the room and say, 'You're the experts! Help us design the system.' But in the future, mechanisms will be created to leverage the wisdom of diverse participants. The new platforms and designs for this process will have questions of ownership and how participation is paid for," he said.

Since competition is becoming more global, a new set of problems is coming to the fore: differential labor costs, cultural differences, variable regulatory requirements, and tax and payment complications.

The personal lives of workers are also changing as new work practices evolve. It is becoming more common for workers to have no fixed work location or permanent office; work is happening at people's homes or in virtual spaces. People's professional and personal lives are starting to blur, and the workday itself is becoming a boundaryless, 24/7 experience. This is adding to workers' stress, which tends to be more mental and emotional than physical in nature.

In this environment of ubiquitous, transparent networks, any employee can publicize information about company behavior and become a social activist, said Gopalakrishnan. He cited the example of Coca-Cola bottlers in India, whom local activists had accused of contaminating water supplies. These charges soon went viral, and international, leading to boycotts of Coca-Cola on college campuses in the United States.

The Disposition of Workers

In the networked environment, the mindset and disposition of workers will matter more than ever. Employers must recognize that they are not just hiring a set of skills, they are hiring people based on their personal temperaments. "In a world of continual and rapid change, maybe the most important things are *dispositions* that allow you to embrace change," said John Seely Brown, Independent Co-Chairman of the Deloitte Center for the Edge.

> **In the networked environment, the mindset and disposition of workers will matter more than ever.**
>
> *John Seely Brown*

Two critical dispositions among the "millennial generation," Brown proposed, are the *questing* disposition—the constant desire to be "on the edge" of breaking developments—and the *productive inquiry* disposition—the passion to probe and question a problem in an attempt to make sense of it and work with it. The questing workers are keenly experimental, audacious and actively searching for the new. Productive-inquiry workers have fierce problem-solving skills and are able to scan, select, analyze, disseminate and discard information on the fly.

Seeing workers through the lens of dispositions helps reframe the challenge facing employers. "You can't *teach* dispositions," said Brown. "You *cultivate* them." Employers cannot simply communicate information to workers; they must provide a hospitable, immersive environment for workers to satisfy their dispositions and talents.

Framing work as a disposition also suggests that work in the future will go beyond 9-to-5 responsibilities. Workers will regard their work lives as an experience, a lifestyle and an identity—not just a paycheck. Employers will have to take cognizance of this fact if they are going to elicit the best from their employees and retain them.

Indeed, said Dwayne Spradlin, President and CEO of InnoCentive, Inc., employers need to recognize that the younger generation of workers, at least among tech enterprises in the U.S., are disdainful towards authority and regimented work processes. They prefer to work in low-structure, improvisational, self-organized environments. They bridle at rules imposed from above. And they are personally committed to social causes.

Spradlin told the story of supervising "hyperactive, very qualified, driven young people" at a business information company in Austin, Texas in the late 1990s. Because he was uncomfortable with the unstructured environment, Spradlin tried to institute all sorts of measurement systems, work plans and deadlines to organize the workplace better. "But every time we would add a required date to fix a problem, particularly for the IT teams," said Spradlin, "they missed the deadline. Every time we would use conventional tools like a deadline for a really big deliverable, or offer a $500 bonus for each worker, the project would crater, time and again."

After a major reassessment of worker incentives, said Spradlin, the company let workers design their own approaches to meet deadlines. Instead of prescribing work processes or mandating "key performance indicators," the firm let work teams self-structure their work and acquire "ownership" of the project. Groups were then judged on outcome-based measures.

This not only enhanced predictability, it lowered costs to the organization and produced better quality products. To cultivate worker loyalty and engagement, the firm also became actively engaged in a variety of philanthropic and social causes such as Habitat for Humanity and fundraising marathons. Spradlin conceded that American high-tech workers may not be representative of global workers, let alone the American workforce, yet he believes these work attitudes are representative of the millennial generation.

How Will Training and Mentoring Happen?

If Spradlin's experience with the millennial generation is a bell-wether, it suggests a certain challenge with no obvious answer: How will the workers of tomorrow obtain the training, mentoring and sense of affiliation and identity that used to happen as a matter of course in "steady jobs"? Where will workers acquire a sense of security and the tools for career development?

In a "free agent" work environment driven by sequential, modular projects, it is not clear how workers will pick up the skills and socialization they will need. There is not necessarily any company that will teach the social protocols of serious business or instill a sense of loyalty and larger purpose.

"You used to get an education from the corporations you worked for," said Tammy Johns of Manpower Inc., "and then you would have some mentorship for life. As skills for work needed to change, corporations would help you learn, and you would get compensated for learning. But now, as we say at Manpower, 'Career management has been outsourced to its owners.' The concept of a single company giving you the skills you need is gone. And higher education is struggling with how rapidly skills are changing."

"Career management has been outsourced to its owners."

Tammy Johns

So how will workers obtain continuous learning, training and mentorship in the future, asked Johns. "Workers of tomorrow need to be able to develop a very clear understanding of what skills they are going to need," she said. One knowledge worker surveyed by Manpower described his plight this way: "I feel like I'm in an airplane at 60,000 feet, destination unknown. I have no idea what skills an employer will need from me in the future."

Manpower has created a website called MyPath to help IT, engineering and accounting professionals assess their skills and manage their careers, and it has innovated with "learning platforms" at Second Life and other immersive online environments to promote workplace collaboration. But if workers will increasingly have to manage their own learning, skills-development and career management, new approaches will be needed.

The core problem may be that education, training and mentorship amount to public goods with no obvious funder. This may be a "market failure," said Thomas Malone of the MIT Center for Collective Intelligence. "Even though creating knowledge and passing it on is of great economic value, the heart of that value-creation isn't economically rewarded in proportion to its value." Tammy Johns recommended new types of private/public partnerships to help address the need for education, training and lifelong learning.

But Kim Taipale noted that it is an open question *where* and *how* these things should occur. "Exceptional competencies occur where human knowledge is created, at the cutting edge, in a community of practice," he said. "This raises an interesting question about where education should happen."

Taipale believes that business itself must become "a platform that supports personal learning environments." It must help workers learn the rules of business and society, transfer "knowledge stories" to new generations of workers, and provide the skills to "exploit knowledge flows."

IV. The Firm of the 21st Century

There is no question that old models of corporate organization and business strategy will persist in the years ahead, especially in underdeveloped nations. Although there will surely be many notable exceptions, only a small percentage of firms in these countries will have the means or foresight to reinvent themselves using information technologies. Most of their workers, too, will likely remain insulated from the trends described above and be grateful for any paid work, period.

And yet in the advanced capitalistic economies of the West, and also in the BRIC countries (Brazil, Russia, India, China), the accelerating innovations in computing, telecommunications, digital networking and related fields will assuredly transform the nature of the firm in the 21st century.

There was general agreement that large corporations using centralized hierarchies and command-and-control management systems will be vulnerable. They will be the least able to adapt their systems to the dynamic changes of a decentralized, networked world. They will also be the most culturally resistant to this new environment.

"To me, we are in a transition moment," said Patrick Gross, Chairman of the Lovell Group, a private investment and advisory firm. "Big organizations tend to operate on a 'Don't change it unless it's broken' philosophy, which is very backward looking. Therefore, by the time that they need to change something, they run into all kinds of problems." Dwayne Spradlin of InnoCentive, Inc. wonders whether "the large company as we know it, as an organizational form, will persist that much longer. Quite frankly, there are not that many terribly big organizations any more. They are either holding companies or lots of smaller companies, which is where the real action is."

However large firms evolve, Spradlin believes they will not be as monolithic in the future: "They're going to be less fixed in structure than they were in the past, and I suspect that everything from the layers of operating systems to the legal frameworks will evaporate." S. Gopalakrishnan of Infosys Technologies Ltd. noted that "there are fewer and fewer large firms in every industrial sector. In technology, there's a consolidation happening, creating larger firms."

> **Large organizations, as traditionally structured, may simply be inadequate to meeting the myriad needs and structural realities of our time.**
>
> *John Rendon*

Large organizations, as traditionally structured, may simply be inadequate to meeting the myriad needs and structural realities of our time. John Rendon, President and CEO of The Rendon Group, Inc., a global strategic communications consulting firm, believes this poses a major challenge to both business and governmental organizations.

He told the story of dozens of young national security analysts, recruited after 9/11, who are deeply frustrated by the bureaucratic norms of their agency. "They feel they could do more *outside* of the institution than they could do *inside* of the institution with every [electronic] toy imaginable.... What happens if the institution is so Industrial Age that it never adapts, and desperately seeks to force the past as a solution-set on an emerging workforce that I consider to be genetically different?" asked Rendon.

Instead of trying to become lifelong employers of people, government agencies should try to embrace the velocity of people's job and career changes, he said. They should enrich their agencies by welcoming the diversity of experiences that job-changing employees bring.

If they are to attract the best employees, work organizations of the future will also need to expand their sense of mission beyond the bottom line, numerous participants argued. "Is the purpose of the firm in the 21st century simply to organize labor and maximize shareholder returns?" asked Dwayne Spradlin. "Or will it need to deliver a greater kind of social good?" Spradlin said that among young employees in the tech sector, a company's social engagement matters a great deal.

Work organizations of the future will also need to expand their sense of mission beyond the bottom line.

But however it reaches out to provide personal and social satisfactions to employees and customers, there is a real challenge in how to *measure* such performance. And however the firm is structured, said Spradlin, it will still have to work "as a structural entity that actually delivers shareholder return and predictability, unless we want to rethink those dimensions altogether."

Can the Big Firm Adapt to the New Environment?

Can the large corporation successfully adapt and compete in the networked environment? That is an open question that elicited a variety of answers.

IBM, with 400,000 employees, is renowned for having reinvented itself at least five different times over the course of its history. Once the leading computer hardware company, IBM now relies predominantly on software and services; 80 percent of its information technology revenues come from selling legacy equipment.

Amazon is also celebrated for making a transformation from an Internet commerce model to a web services model. When asked how this dramatic change was orchestrated, John Seely Brown, who sits on Amazon's board of directors, noted that Amazon had already been building web services for internal purposes; it then realized that it might be able to sell them to the outside world, as a business proposition, which it proceeded to do.

Aside from IBM and Amazon, Michel Chui, Senior Fellow at the McKinsey Global Institute of McKinsey & Company, is skeptical of the ability of large firms to change their business models. "In practice I've really only seen companies change their business models in small startups. I don't know how a big organization can flexibly change its business model quickly in that way."

Robert Morris, Vice President of Services Research for IBM Research, agreed that "transformation is the hardest thing." It can occur through external disruptions or through induced internal disruptions, but the latter are quite difficult to pull off. "It's all about talent management, and it's very hard to transform talent," he said. "The easy way to do it is through acquisitions and through putting new people in new places."

Still, conference participants offered a number of ideas for how large corporations might try to adapt to the networked world.

One of the most counterintuitive ideas is "employees first, customers second," which is the title of a book by Vineet Nayar, the CEO of HCL Technologies, an information technology firm. As described by Shami Khorana, President of HCL America, "Everything in the company has to revolve around empowerment and transparency." Management must strive to "create value for the employee," so that the employee will be motivated to interact with customers (both "internal customers" within the company and conventional customers) in honest, effective ways. The point is to improve the interface between the customer and the company, the so-called "value zone."

CEO Nayar was able to transform HCL Technologies over the course of several years without instituting employee satisfaction programs, massive restructurings or major technology initiatives. As he describes it in *Employees First, Customers Second* (Harvard Business Press, 2010), Nayer spoke bluntly about the company's troubled situation to employees around the world. He opened up the company's books and shared that financial information freely, which in turn spurred employees and managers to begin asking hard questions of each other.

HCL Technologies also "inverted the pyramid" of the company structure so that management and all supporting functions served the employees first—who, as a result, became more effective and motivated about their work. Finally, Nayar "destroyed the office of the CEO" by "transferring responsibility for change from the office of the CEO to the employees in the value zone." The idea was to make leadership and responsibility more distributed, and less dependent on a single CEO or corps of elite executives.

In this vision of a large company, "managers are all about creating value for employees," said Khorana. "They help provide context and meaning for employees." He cited the story of the bricklayer who in one scenario is "laying bricks" and in another conceptualization of his work is "building a cathedral." The CEO needs to help employees see how they are building a cathedral.

Dwayne Spradlin offered his own story of promoting distributed leadership at a demoralized customer service department at a large tech company. In the face of indifference from other company departments, Spradlin urged the staff to emulate Winston Churchill's resolve and leadership to force change within the company—a process that fed on itself as small victories were won. The internal disruptions proved to be effective and changed the morale and effectiveness of the customer service department.

Kim Taipale of the Stilwell Center for Advanced Studies in Science and Technology Policy said that the way to transform a static organization into a dynamic, flexible one is to foster internal disruptions. He said that, as a young investment banker in the 1980s, he was once singled out by a partner to play the role of internal disrupter. Taipale was using computer spreadsheets to evaluate deals at a time when the prevailing custom among senior partners was to rely on back-of-the-envelope calculations. As a Young Turk, Taipale could play a disruptive role that was seen as inappropriate to the senior partners.

Another way that large firms can instigate internal change is "by creating multiple agents of growth within the firm," said S. Gopalakrishnan of Infosys Technologies Ltd. Instead of trying to instigate "one big change," companies should empower "second- or third-tier leaders to undertake multiple change initiatives," which they will usually regard as their opportunity to become "tier-one leaders."

As a former change management consultant, Tim H. El-Hady, Director of Business Planning and Operations at Microsoft U.K. Ltd., believes that any change must be articulated through a vision that people can buy into: "What are we trying to achieve? What is the role of everybody in the transition process?" A vision is important because it can emotionally engage employees. But advancing a vision can only be achieved through humility and consultation, El-Hady stressed. The process must be "very clear, open and truth-seeking" so that everyone will participate and be willing to support the plans that are eventually adopted.

As these stories imply, transformation within large companies depends a great deal on leadership. "I think we need to think about innovation in management models, in leadership models," said Maryam Alavi of the Goizueta Business School at Emory University. "In business schools, we still teach the more traditional, classical models of leadership and management. When they are superimposed on today's realities, they don't really accommodate the challenges we face."

One way to reorient management is to focus on the long term, said Robert Morris. At IBM, he said, the company has been providing five-year estimates for its earnings. This reorients the attention of employees and shareholders to the company's strategic priorities.

Another management model is to regard the internal relations of a firm itself as a network, so that the various "silos" of the organization can more freely interact with each other, exchange information and collaborate. This is important because, "if information technology increases the metabolic rate of information processing within organizations," said Alavi, "then you need to come up with innovative management models."

However one looks at it, large corporations will have trouble adapting to the networked environment, and many may not survive. As Thomas Malone put it, "We should probably expect that the main way that this transition will occur is with new companies—startups—that are different from the beginning, rather than old companies that are transformed."

The Firm as a Talent-Management Organization

If the business enterprises of the Sloan Age were about orchestrating diverse production activities and centrally managing work rules and norms, most participants agreed the firms of the 21st century will mostly be about talent management.

A good business plan and available capital are no substitute for a talented workforce whose members passionately buy into the vision. Spradlin calls it "the single core differentiator and probably predictor of success in organizations."

... the firms of the 21st century will mostly be about talent management.

When talent is highly fluid and moving in and out of organizations, access to talent becomes a serious challenge. So how to assure reliable access to talent? Trust and transparency are important in attracting the best workers. Clarity of mission and purpose are becoming important in galvanizing people to contribute their best. "It's not just about acquiring, developing and retaining talent," said Spradlin. "It's about doing that with style and purpose." To focus people's attention and earn their loyalty, it helps to organize work among smaller teams and pods, so that people can feel a sense of ownership and control in how they structure their work. A sense of passion and mission among employees is key to reducing turnover, he said.

For the software entrepreneur Bill Coleman, the most important ingredient in a successful startup today is the initial people who are hired. "All I really need to own is the core competencies," he said; most of the other costs of starting a business, especially one based on intellectual property, are relatively low.

"So my principles are simple," said Coleman. "I call it the 'three Vs: vision, value and values.' You have to have a *vision* of how you're going to transform the marketplace, and how you are going to add *value* for customers that is totally differentiable, compelling and urgent. And the final one, *values*, is obvious. It's all about people. The only people you hire are the core competencies."

Coleman sees the CEO and management as "coaches" attempting to elicit the best from employees: "You want to set up a system that breaks work down so that the people making decisions—about products and channels of distribution—are the ones closest to the products and channels, and they are held accountable. On the software development side, people work in the smallest possible teams—of no more than six to ten people—so that they 'own' what results in the marketplace."

"If you do it right," said Coleman, "the company will always be adapting, always changing course, because you will be there ahead of the market, not when the wave hits. Even more, you will be segmenting your customers as they pull you into different products."

A firm is not just about talent management, objected John Seely Brown. "It's equally about talent *development.*" By that, he means that firms must provide a learning environment if they are going to attract and retain the best employees.

He cited the example of the Chinese company Li & Fung, which got its start in the apparel industry by providing a networked platform to manufacture clothing for apparel designers using more than 10,000 business partners in 40 countries.[11] Operating as a loose but highly responsive and fluid network, Li & Fung coordinates nearly everything in the supply-network process, from raw material sourcing and production to logistics and quality checks.

Li & Fung operates under a so-called 30/30 rule, which guarantees the companies that belong to its network that Li & Fung will buy at least 30 percent of their output, but they must look to other customers for at least 30 percent of their output. That is, Li & Fung will never pay for more than 70 percent of the vendor's output, lest the vendor become too captive and subservient to Li & Fung.

This arrangement cultivates trust among network partners, and virtually forces Li & Fung partners to learn and innovate all the time. The 30/30 rule also assures that all vendors will work with Li & Fung's competitors, which means that new ideas and market signals quickly circle back to Li & Fung management. The company acquires a constant, efficient source of market intelligence and early cues for adapting its competitive practices.

This loosely networked arrangement has dramatically lowered transaction costs among companies in the network, said Brown. The company reaps $1 million per employee in revenue—in a business based on high-volume, low-margin work.

Is the Network the Successor to the Firm?

Whether it is talent-management or risk-management, one of the clear implications for the future is that "the firm is essentially moving to a platform," said Kim Taipale. "The firm is moving to become an enabling environment in an ecosystem, whose goal is to create value in some market niche. The firm will become about building a platform where people can create value, and the firm will then capture some part of that value stream."

"The firm is essentially moving to a platform."

Kim Taipale

This theme is explored in a reading for the conference, "Enterprise 2.0: The Dawn of Emergent Collaboration," which describes how corporate intranets are becoming a "constantly changing structure built by distributed, autonomous peers—a collaborative platform that reflects the way work really gets done."[12] The author, Andrew P. McAfee, notes, "Current platforms are not doing a good job of capturing knowledge. New platforms focus not on capturing knowledge itself, but rather on the *practices* and *outputs* of knowledge workers." By making the practices and outputs more visible, companies can more readily exploit them for competitive purposes.

As described earlier, the pharmaceutical industry realized years ago that a "virtual pharma company" was an attractive way to minimize risk and leverage distributed knowledge. "It's a more effective form," explained Dwayne Spradlin, "because you're compartmentalizing investment and risk management. That's all that a big company becomes—a management of risk and capital. It sets a strategy and makes choices about what molecules and diseases they are going to investigate. I think you're beginning to see this more and more."

As a firm's activities become more integrated with a network platform, the boundaries that once defined a firm will become more porous and blurry. The relationships among people within the company and with "outsiders" will become more ambiguous. In a sense, the many vendors who use eBay and the participants in InnoCentive's research queries are "part of the company" even though they are not employees in a strict sense. They are participants on a shared network platform.

Kim Taipale calls these "3C" platforms. At any given time, any two entities on the network platform will be engaged in competition, cooperation and conflict simultaneously. "Firms are going to open their borders, and it will mean that your clients and competitors are going to be 'inside' your network," said Taipale. "You're going to have to figure out how to work in that environment."

If the network is going to generate value, it will need to support adaptation among players in the network, he continued. It will need to foster entrepreneurship and "edge ventures." Indeed, the market itself is going to move away from "core deciding" by large market players, and move to the hosting of "market forces on the edge."

V. The Social Implications of Globally Organized Work

If the future of work holds many great possibilities for businesses that are creative and flexible, it also holds many formidable and frightening risks for society. The biggest dangers are greater inequalities of wealth and potentially destructive social polarization. These trends make it imperative that government, education and social institutions learn how to respond to the emerging networked environment.

The biggest dangers are greater inequalities of wealth and potentially destructive social polarization.

Social alienation is a significant risk. Kim Taipale, Founder and Executive Director of the Stilwell Center for Advanced Studies in Science and Technology Policy, showed a music video from the 1990 movie *Joe Versus the Volcano* depicting an alienated young man who works in a dreary, routinized office job at which he is always fantasizing about escaping to a tropical island. The soundtrack is an Eric Burdon version of "Sixteen Tons," the Merle Travis song about the alienation of coal miners in the 1930s, now applied to an advanced, high-tech workplace.

Taipale argued that while network platforms offer a greater equality of access in principle, a network in practice tends to produce a "power-law distribution," in which a small minority of players tend to dominate the rest—a "winner take all" scenario. "The Long Tail may represent 'opportunity' for businesses," said Taipale, "but as a social matter, it represents a serious problem. How do you manage the inequalities implicit in the Long Tail? If the power law governs networks, leading to winner-take-all scenarios, then how will government or some other mechanism allocate the spoils of greater productivity?"

There are several levels of inequality arising at work. There are those workers who are able to use information technology and reap some of its benefits and those who cannot. Among those in the first group, there are those who are empowered by the technology as creative knowledge workers or managers and those who are stuck in socially alienating entry-level and dead-end jobs. How shall educational institutions respond? Governments? International bodies for commerce, social welfare, the environment and human rights?

Mircea Geoana, President of the Romanian Senate and President, Aspen Institute Romania, is wary about the future: "I believe inequalities are here to stay, and I believe that the shift in global work and global economies will increase tensions at the global level. I don't think we are heading toward a peaceful, serene world. We are now in an economic war; this is what is going on. In terms of its global implications, this economic war has the magnitude of the Second World War."

> **"We are now in an economic war; this is what is going on. In terms of its global implications, this economic war has the magnitude of the Second World War."**
>
> *Mircea Geoana*

Geoana identified three specific problems that are likely to intensify in coming years: lack of access to education, troubles in renegotiating the "social contract" between citizens and governments, and difficulties in revamping systems of taxation and redistribution that are necessary to pay for public goods and assure minimal standards of social well-being.

European governments are currently grappling with the future of their social contracts with citizens and the specific services they provide, said Geoana, who noted that there are in fact many variations of the European social contract—Anglo-Saxon; Scandinavian; the so-called Rhine model of Germany, France, Belgium, and Luxembourg; Mediterranean; and those of the former communist countries. In each instance, global competition is challenging the scope of government powers and the financing of services.

This raises some difficult, unresolved questions: How can governments regulate markets while protecting the environment and citizens, and how can they provide education as a public good even as tax revenues dwindle?

"If we have a tier of global elite producing most of the returns on investment, how is this going to affect taxation and the redistribution of wealth in the society?" asked Geoana. "How can we provide for the whole planet? We'll have ten billion inhabitants—and all of them will be doing highly cognitive work? No."

Geoana characterized the recent financial crisis as "one of the most intense periods of global competition and realignment we have witnessed, probably in the history of humankind. Nobody anticipated that the economic downturn would change the world so quickly and have such intense geopolitical implications." Geoana finds it plausible that the Gross Domestic Product of the West could be eclipsed by that of the emerging powers of the world within 20 years.

However current trends unfold, Geoana sees the need for rethinking "the architecture of this new world." Groups like the G-20 and G-7 may have to be enlarged to accommodate other countries, he said, and "the relationships between the big-deficit countries and the surplus countries" will have to be re-aligned. All of these changes will be complicated by the intensifying global competition for resources now underway, which is directed not only at energy and natural resources but at human talent. Many smaller countries, such as Romania, are experiencing a serious brain-drain of talented professionals, Geoana said. More medical doctors and nurses leave the country than graduate from health care training facilities each year, for instance.

Geoana fears for the "civic fabric" and "social harmony" of countries as the power of traditional counterforces—trade unions and nongovernmental organizations—declines, making it more difficult for governments to perform their traditional functions.

"What will be the new 'commanding heights' of a successful society in the 21st century?" Geoana asked. "We are trying to find a new answer" because the free-market vision promoted by the Chicago School of Economics, Ronald Reagan and Margaret Thatcher is now obsolete.

And yet the Keynesian social welfare model is experiencing major difficulties, too. Geoana believes that it is an illusion to think that information technologies and a knowledge economy can generate a global middle class in a simple, linear way. The big challenge in building a new society, he insisted, is finding a way to preserve social cohesiveness and trust under the immense pressures of disruptive economic and technological forces.

Geoana confessed to "an intense sense of danger" because of "new tensions in key places of the tectonic plates of the planet. There could be open war, new competition, violence, terrorism, or something else," he said, "but you can be sure that the realignments of finance, political power, access to resources, national identities and global identities will matter."

Madeleine Albright, the former U.S. Secretary of State, now the Chair of Albright Capital Management LLC and the Albright Stonebridge Group, shared many of Geoana's concerns, but called herself "an optimist who likes to worry a lot." She added: "We are at a moment where there is no faith in our institutional structures, whether domestic or international. You see it across the board—the G-20, G-7, the United Nations. The question is, "What are the institutional structures that can move us from here to there?"

> **"The gap is more dangerous because of information technology— because the poor know exactly what the rich have."**
>
> *Madeleine Albright*

But one of the deepest challenges, said Albright, is "the division between the rich and poor. By absolute numbers there are fewer poor people in the world today, primarily because China has lifted so many people out of poverty. But the gap is growing, and the gap is more dangerous because of information technology—because the poor know exactly what the rich have." Poor people see that they are disenfranchised and disadvantaged relatively. Albright sees "the beginnings of class warfare in various places" right now.

An article in the *Wall Street Journal* by Robert Frank asked the question, Do the Rich Need the Rest of America?[13] Frank proposed the possibility that "the economic fate of Richistan [his term for the super-rich] seems increasingly separate from the fate of the U.S." Citing policy analyst Michael Lind, Frank writes that "the wealthy increasingly earn their fortunes with overseas labor, selling to overseas consumers and managing financial transactions that have little to do with the rest of the U.S." According to Lind, "a member of the elite can make money from factories in China that sell to consumers in India, while relying entirely or almost entirely on immigrant servants at one of several homes around the country."

Meanwhile, the disenfranchised poor who are not well-served, or served at all, by their governments, may turn to extremist movements. S. Gopalakrishnan reported that in India, the Naxalites, a movement of Marxists who believe in revolutionary change through violence, control large parts of the country. "The movement has instituted its own parallel government, tax system and sets of rules," he said, "because they don't see government benefiting them. So they're turning to alternate forms of justice."

Social polarization and lack of education can also undermine the economic system in many countries, said Robert Morris of IBM Research, and it is beginning to pose significant technological, infrastructure and security problems. In particular, he noted that there is a significant portion of the world's population who are largely disenfranchised from the benefits of economic growth.

How Should Governments Respond?

How might governments respond to this daunting array of economic, technological and social pressures? Any answer, said Kim Taipale, requires us to recognize that the very premises of the nation-state themselves are under intense pressure from the Internet and digital technologies. "All of our existing organizations and rules, from nation-states to firms, essentially assume the inefficiencies of the old ways of doing things," he said. The nation-state is premised on the basic rootedness of human beings in a fixed territory and on language barriers preventing people from communicating with other peoples.

"Nation-states came into being to manage those inefficiencies," said Taipale, "and now those inefficiencies are being challenged." He added that they are being challenged not just with new information flows, but with human migration, capital flows and many other things. The centrifugal energies of information technologies and global commerce are breaking down the "Westphalian premises" of the nation-state, which cannot exercise absolute control over what occurs within its own boundaries—*viz.*, how people may communicate, how resources may be exploited, how capital may flow and how the economy is managed.

The question we should be asking, said Taipale, is, "What is the core competency of a government in a world where the 'old business model' is not necessarily relevant any more?"

His answer is that government should regard itself as a platform for human and social development. And just as firms try to capture some of the value generated by network platforms to sustain themselves, so governments need to gather some value from their platforms and reinvest that value for their own constituencies. Taipale conceded that it is not self-evident how governments can extract taxation and reinvest it constructively when so many flows of information, capital and people are beyond its control.

There was general consensus among conference participants, however, that governments need to try to mitigate inequality and provide public goods that the market cannot. Government can also adopt information technologies to improve the efficiency and effectiveness of its own services. In many countries, said Robert Morris, "Services quality is in a state of absolute breakdown, especially in the provision of health, education and government services.... We must do things differently, and one major lever is to increase the quality of services offered." One major forum at which such things are being discussed is the annual Government 2.0 conference held in Washington, D.C. each September.[14]

It would be highly useful if governments around the world began to share knowledge and best practices about the future of work, said John Rendon, President and CEO of The Rendon Group, Inc. "We're desperately trying to return to the past, when things made sense. But the world has moved on, and we haven't. We need to understand that the status quo has changed globally in education and in business practices."

There was consensus, too, that international institutions and cooperation must change in order to take account of the increased connectedness and mobility among people. "The mobility of people across nations and migration to cities are creating new social tensions," said S. Gopalakrishnan, "because the numbers are unprecedented." But there are no institutional mechanisms to make sure that the immigrants are welcome or not welcome. Within the next 10 to 20 years, added Michael Chui of McKinsey & Company, it is estimated that another 100 cities will see their populations top one million people, creating enormous pressures on civic infrastructure and government services, not to mention basic social order.[15]

A number of participants urged a greater harmonization of regulatory regimes across international boundaries, so that compliance with various labor-related laws would be less cumbersome. For example, many laws governing wages, employment standards, taxes and retirement are highly inconsistent or outmoded, said Marion McGovern, Co-Founder of M Squared Consulting, Inc.

Similarly, an international infrastructure to enable easy payment to employees and contractors across national borders is needed, said Tammy Johns, Senior Vice President at Manpower. For instance, when workers outside of the United States participate in Amazon's Mechanical Turk, they are paid in Amazon.com gift certificates rather than the official currency of their country.

In response, Thomas Malone of the MIT Center for Collective Intelligence proposed an innovative scheme for dealing with incompatible regulatory regimes for employment: "an international regulatory regime to facilitate remote work, telework or virtual work." Malone likens the idea to international tax treaties that assure the collection of tax revenues from citizens of one nationality performing work in another nation. The point would be to harmonize, or at least find some universal accommodation, among the diverse income tax and labor laws as they apply to online work. Individuals would be able to pursue work across national borders and enhance economic growth while governments would be able to assure minimal work standards and reap tax benefits.

There was keen interest in this idea as well as rueful acknowledgment of its great complexities. Yet the idea may also offer a valuable test case for Taipale's idea that "the successor to the firm is the network." The challenge, said Taipale, can be summarized thus: "For distance work across national borders, what is the governance structure that lowers interaction costs so that individuals can plug into it, and yet governments can feel like they're getting their share of the pie?"

In sum, as governments face the conflicting pressures in the networked environment, they must try to facilitate trans-border employment and commerce while finding the means to reinvent education and other government services essential to their own citizenries.

National governments and regional governance will remain important forces in solving this quandary, said Robert Morris, if only because they create some very fundamental and necessary institutions. Governments play vital roles in supporting education, research and infrastructure, and in crafting immigration policies that ensure a diversity of talent.

But it remains an open question how governments will come to understand the new paradigm of networked work, let alone adapt to it through new structures and policies. One especially vexing issue is how to assure accountability in a networked environment. Governments and organizations need to be accountable; traditionally, we look to some individual "leader" or executive. But in a network that is quasi-autonomous and self-organizing, how does anyone assert control, accept responsibility or provide accountability?

These realities make it all the more important that we develop "network governance protocol structures," as Kim Taipale put it, so that there can be certain structural design features to foster trust and accountability for interactions on a network. For example, if we wish to have global contract enforcement and global security—to prevent email scams or destructive software viruses—we need to develop appropriate and effective protocols. "The problem is, How do you get those standards applied across the board, so that everybody is playing by the same rules?" Taipale asked.

An interesting test case may be the Vermont "virtual corporations law," which provides state chartering of virtual corporations much as Delaware provides an attractive state law for chartering multinational corporations.[16] But how does one assure that the standards of the Vermont law, or any such law for virtual entities, is universally recognized and enforced? That is the scaling problem for government in the networked environment.

John Seely Brown noted that the future will require a great deal of institutional innovation if we are to meet the challenges of the networked environment. When he was asked what innovation led to more wealth creation than anything else, Brown said that he was presumably expected to name the microprocessor. But in fact, he said, the more significant innovation was not technological but institutional: the limited liability corporation.

So, today, he said, we need to investigate new forms of institutional management that can more effectively deal with the emerging challenges. He cited the work in this regard by Yochai Benkler, a law professor at Harvard, and by John Clippinger, head of The Law Lab at Harvard's Berkman Center for Internet and Society. Clippinger is currently exploring the idea of an "open governance" project that would investigate new institutional models of governance.

In that regard, David Bollier, the rapporteur and long-time student of "the commons" as a paradigm of governance and resource management, suggested that "technology now allows for all sorts of self-organized governance to collectively manage shared resources, mostly in a non-market fashion." He cited open-source software, Wikipedia, collaborative websites and wikis, and social networking platforms as examples. All rely upon online communities of shared purpose to generate serious economic value outside of traditional market structures in socially satisfying ways.

...commons-based governance holds great promise for dealing with social alienation and inequality.

David Bollier

These sorts of commons-based governance hold great promise for dealing with social alienation and inequality, Bollier suggested, while also providing stable resource management. He cited the work of Professor Elinor Ostrom of Indiana University, who won the 2009 Nobel Prize in Economics for her pioneering research about how commons regimes manage natural resources sustainably and effectively.

How Should Education Change?

A related challenge is the transformation of education. There was wide consensus that existing educational institutions are generally deficient in providing quality education to the masses in ways that recognize the new realities of the marketplace and digital networks. Although it was beyond the scope of the conference to "solve" this massive, complicated issue, there were a number of specific suggestions for how to reform public education.

Among them: better incentives for teachers and greater specialization in instruction (Tim H. El-Hady); a new focus on continuous education and teaching by great teachers (Olivier Mellerio); new curricula that "encourage the art of dialogue and collaboration" (Marion McGovern); and the coordination of education with private job needs (John Rendon).

Another key theme was the importance of internationalizing education. American schools, in particular, should develop ties to universities around the world, many participants urged. This should occur at all levels of education, from kindergarten through 12th grade, and at all levels of higher education.

"The U.S. Secretary of Education could convene the top 50 universities in the United States and urge their presidents to develop relationships with universities in other parts of the world, at a sub-regional level, and to make a commitment to lifelong learning," said John Rendon. With leadership from the White House and private sector, the first five or ten schools to make such a commitment could be recognized and rewarded in some fashion as a way of encouraging other schools to emulate them. Universities could also leverage their alumni to participate in the process.

"We are not preparing business school students for the new environment," said Maryam Alavi of the Goizueta Business School at Emory University. "We don't teach our graduates how to learn." She believes business schools ought to teach critical thinking and foster global awareness by instigating an international collaboration among business schools, going well beyond "study abroad" programs that last only a semester or two.

Kim Taipale stressed that any attempt to internationalize education should not just be focused on a "push model" of simple school affiliations with a network. The endeavor should be conceived of as a "pull model" that establishes network standards and best practices that then attracts an emergent network of schools. New patterns and practices of education should emerge from the network over time, rather than existing institutions simply "pushing" a prescribed set of programs and activities.

Tim El-Hady, Director of Business Planning and Operations for Microsoft U.K. Ltd, proposed that it should be a mandatory qualification for membership in international bodies, whether the World Trade Organization or the United Nations, that a nation have "a viable social entrepreneurship program" to stimulate focused action on social and economic problems. The goal should be to nurture a new kind of global citizenship, which in turn could influence policy efforts in education, work and commerce. "The well-being of mankind, its peace and security, are unattainable unless and until its unity is firmly established," said El-Hady, quoting Bahá'u'lláh, the Prophet Founder of the Bahá'í Faith. One enterprising model for social entrepreneurship, noted Charles Firestone, Executive Director of the Aspen Institute Communications and Society Program, is a website called HopePlus.org, which functions as "a kind of online Peace Corps."

Conclusion

The questions raised in the course of this conference were far more numerous than the answers. Still, the spirited dialogue illuminated many murky corners of a vast constellation of interconnected issues: the power of distributed knowledge and open platforms, the profound transformations that they are bringing to market structures and business organizations, the necessary shifts in business strategy and worker skills in the new environment, and the barely recognized challenges facing governments in adapting to the new environment.

The transformation underway is so difficult to grapple with because the changes are occurring on multiple levels at the same time in a confusing, interconnected web. People's everyday habits and social practices are changing as the technology is evolving. And those changes are co-evolving with institutional structures, the economic logic of networks and diverse cultures on an international stage.

Government and public policy can play a tremendously helpful role in guiding the forces that are emerging. But historically, government and public policy have tended to be more reactive and short-term oriented, not pro-active and visionary. This is an ominous reality because larger governance structures are desperately needed to assure benign, if not constructive, network protocols and to prevent dominant companies or industries from compromising the promise of open platforms and digital networking. New sorts of government leadership are needed to address social inequality, education and training, and improvements in government services. New sorts of self-organized, commons-based governance regimes can provide useful group provisioning and coordination as well.

There is a keen imperative, in short, for serious institutional innovation. There is a need for new forms of governance and a renegotiated social contract between governments and citizens. These are epic challenges, of course, but simply naming them and understanding their key implications are necessary first steps to tackling them.

Notes

1. Robert Reich, *The Future of Success* (New York: Knopf, 2001).

2. Ibid., 95.

3. John Hagel III, John Seely Brown, and Lang Davison, *The Power of Pull: How Small Moves, Smartly Made, Can Set Big Things in Motion* (New York: Basic Books, 2010). See also the report of the 2005 Aspen Institute Information Technology Roundtable: *When Push Comes to Pull: The new Economy and Culture of Networking Technology* (Washington, DC: The Aspen Institute, 2006).

4. Hagel et al, *The Power of Pull*, 39.

5. Jacque Bughin, James Manyika, and Roger Roberts, "New Degrees of Management Freedom: Challenging Sloan Age Business Orthodoxies," *McKinsey Technology Initiative Perspective* (October 2008).

6. Amazon's Mechanical Turk, https://www.mturk.com/mturk/welcome

7. "List of Crowdsourcing Projects," *Wikipedia*, last modified November 12, 2010, https://secure.wikimedia.org/wikipedia/en/wiki/List_of_crowdsourcing_projects.

8. InnoCentive profiled at length in Henry Chesbrough, *Open Business Models: How to Thrive in the New Innovation Landscape* (Cambridge: Harvard Business School Press, 2006), 141–148.

9. Thomas W. Malone, Joanne Yates, and Robert I. Benjamin, "Electronic Markets and Electronic Hierarchies," *Communications of the ACM* 30, no. 6 (June 1987): 484–497.

10. Thomas W. Malone, *The Future of Work: How the New Order of Business Will Shape Your Organization, Your Management Style, and Your Life* (Boston: Harvard Business School Press, 2004).

11. See Hagel et al, *The Power of Pull* , 83–85.

12. Andrew P. McAfee, "Enterprise 2.0: The Dawn of Emergent Collaboration," *MIT Sloan Management Review* 47, no. 3, (April 2006), 21–28, http://sloanreview.mit.edu/the-magazine/ articles/2006/spring/47306/enterprise-the-dawn-of-emergent-collaboration.

13. Robert Frank, "Do the Rich Need the Rest of America?" *The Wealth Report* (blog) *Wall Street Journal*, August 2, 2010, http://blogs.wsj.com/wealth/2010/08/02/do-the-rich-even-need-the-rest-of-america-anymore.

14. Government 2.0 Summit, http://www.gov2summit.com/gov2010

15. See, e.g., Richard Dobbs, "Megacities," *Foreign Policy* (September/October 2010), http://www. foreignpolicy.com/articles/2010/08/16/prime_numbers_megacities, which describes how migration from the countryside to cities will result in 289 cities in India and China having more than one million residents by 2030. http://www.foreignpolicy.com/articles/2010/08/16/ prime_numbers_megacities

16. Vermont Virtual Corporations law, http://www.sec.state.vt.us/corps/corpindex.htm.

APPENDIX

The Nineteenth Annual Aspen Institute
Roundtable on Information Technology

The Future of Work

Aspen, Colorado • August 3–6, 2010

Roundtable Participants

Maryam Alavi
Vice Dean, and The John and
 Lucy Cook Chair of Information
 Strategy
Goizueta Business School
Emory University

Madeleine K. Albright
Chair
Albright Stonebridge Group
Albright Capital Management LLC

David Bollier
Independent Journalist and
 Consultant
Onthecommons.org

John Seely Brown
Independent Co-Chairman
Deloitte Center for the Edge

Jacques Bughin
Director
McKinsey & Company, Inc.,
 Belgium

Michael Chui
Senior Fellow
McKinsey Global Institute
McKinsey & Company, Inc.

William T. Coleman III
Partner
Alsop Louie Partners

Tim H. El-Hady
Director of Business Planning
 and Operations
Microsoft U.K. Ltd.

Charles M. Firestone
Executive Director
Communications and Society
 Program
The Aspen Institute

Mircea Geoana
President of the Romanian Senate
 and
President, Aspen Institute Romania

S. Gopalakrishnan
Chief Executive Officer and
 Managing Director
Infosys Technologies Ltd.

Patrick Gross
Chairman
The Lovell Group

Paul Inouye
Partner
Perella Weinberg Partners

Note: Titles and affiliations are as of the date of the conference.

Peter Jackson
Chief Scientist and
Vice-President, Corporate
 Research & Development
Thomson Reuters

Tammy Johns
Senior Vice President, Innovation
 & Workforce Solutions
Manpower, Inc.

Shami Khorana
President
HCL America, Inc.

Thomas W. Malone
Director, MIT Center for
 Collective Intelligence, and
Patrick J. McGovern Professor of
 Management
Sloan School of Management
Massachusetts Institute of
 Technology

James Manyika
Director
McKinsey Global Institute, and
Senior Partner
McKinsey & Company, Inc.

Marion McGovern
Co-Founder
M Squared Consulting Inc.

Robert Morris
Vice President, Services Research
IBM Research

Jerry Murdock
Co-Founder and Managing
 Director
Insight Venture Partners

John Rendon
President and Chief Executive
 Officer
The Rendon Group, Inc.

Dwayne Spradlin
President and Chief Executive
 Officer
InnoCentive, Inc.

Kim Taipale
Founder and Executive Director
The Stilwell Center for Advanced
 Studies in Science and
 Technology Policy

*Aspen Institute International
Participants:*

Olivier Mellerio
Institut Aspen France
 and
President, Mellerio International

Carlo Scognamiglio
Honorary Chairman
Aspen Institute Italia

Staff:

Peter T. Keefer
Communications Manager and
 Web Producer
Communications and Society
 Program
The Aspen Institute

Note: Titles and affiliations are as of the date of the conference.

About the Author

David Bollier (www.bollier.org) is an author, activist, blogger and consultant who has served as rapporteur for Aspen Institute Communications and Society conferences for more than 20 years.

Much of Bollier's work over the past ten years has been devoted to exploring the commons as a new paradigm of economics, politics and culture. He pursues this work in collaboration with a variety of domestic and international partners, often under the auspices of the Commons Strategy Group, which he recently co-founded, and through his blog, Bollier.org.

Bollier's first book on the commons, *Silent Theft: The Private Plunder of Our Commons Wealth*, is a far-ranging survey of market enclosures of shared resources, from public lands and the airwaves to creativity and knowledge. *Brand Name Bullies: The Quest to Own and Control Culture* documents the vast expansion of copyright and trademark law over the past generation. Bollier's latest book, *Viral Spiral: How the Commoners Built a Digital Republic of Their Own*, describes the rise of free software, free culture, and the movements behind open business models, open science, open educational resources and new modes of Internet-enabled citizenship.

Since 1984, Bollier has worked with American television writer/ producer Norman Lear and served as Senior Fellow at the Norman Lear Center at the USC Annenberg School for Communication. Bollier is also co-founder and board member of Public Knowledge, a Washington policy advocacy organization dedicated to protecting the information commons. Bollier lives in Amherst, Massachusetts.

Previous Publications
from the Aspen Institute
Roundtable on Information Technology

The Promise and Peril of Big Data (2009)
David Bollier, rapporteur

Ever-rising floods of data are being generated by mobile networking, cloud computing and other new technologies. At the same time, continued innovations use advanced correlation techniques to analyze them, and the process and payoff can be both encouraging and alarming. The Eighteenth Annual Roundtable on Information Technology sought to understand the implications of the emergence of "Big Data" and new techniques of inferential analysis. Roundtable participants explored ways these inferential technologies can positively affect medicine, business and government, and they examined the social perils they pose. The report of the 2009 Roundtable, written by David Bollier, summarizes the insights of the Roundtable and concludes with its analysis of the financial sector from the perspective of Big Data, particularly how massive transparency, common reporting languages and open source analytics might greatly relieve the problems of systemic risk. 2010, 56 pages, ISBN Paper 0-89843-516-1, $12 per copy, Free download at www.aspeninstitute.org.

Identity in the Age of Cloud Computing: The next-generation Internet's impact on business, governance and social-interaction (2008)
J.D. Lasica, rapporteur

The Seventeenth Annual Roundtable on Information Technology brought together 28 leaders and experts from the ICT, financial, government, academic, and public policy sectors to better understand the implications of cloud computing and, where appropriate, to suggest policies for the betterment of society. Participants discussed the migration of information, software and identity into the Cloud and explored the transformative possibilities of this new computing paradigm for culture, business and personal interaction. The report of the roundtable, written by J.D. Lasica, offers insights from the roundtable and includes a set of policy recommendations and advice for the new presidential adminis-tration. 2009, 98 pages, ISBN Paper 0-89843-505-6, $12 per copy.

Beyond the Edge: Decentralized Co-creation of Value (2007)
David Bollier, rapporteur

The 2007 Roundtable convened 27 leaders to analyze the current and future social and economic impacts the co-creation of knowledge across networks made possible with new communications and information technologies. While collaborative engagement encourages increased pro-ductivity and creativity, it can also lead to mass chaos from the co-creation process. The roundtable participants discussed what separates successes from failures in the new collaborative era by reviewing business and organi-zational models and the implications of new models. 2007, 64 pages, ISBN Paper 0-89843-481-5, $12.00 per copy.

The Mobile Generation: Global Transformations at the Cellular Level (2006)
J.D. Lasica, rapporteur

The 2006 Roundtable examined the profound changes ahead as a result of the convergence of wireless technologies and the Internet. The Roundtable addressed the technological and behavioral changes already taking place in the United States and other parts of the world as a result of widespread and innovative uses of wireless devices; the trends in these behaviors, especially with the younger generation; and what this could mean for life values in the coming decade. The Roundtable tackled new economic and business models for communications entities, social and political ramifications, and the implications for leaders in all parts of the world. 66 pages, ISBN Paper 0-89843-466-1, $12.00 per copy.

When Push Comes to Pull: The New Economy and Culture of Networking Technology (2005)
David Bollier, rapporteur

The author considers how communications, economics, business, cul-tural, and social institutions are changing from mass production to an indi-vidualized "pull" model. *When Push Comes to Pull* describes the coexistence of both push (top down or hierarchical) and pull (bottom up or networked) models—how they interact, evolve, and overlay each other in the networked information economy. The report explores the application of "pull" to the worlds of business and economics; the content and intellectual property industries; the emergence of an economy of the commons; and personal and social dynamics, including leadership in a pull world. It also touches on the application of the pull model to learning systems; the military, in the form of network-centric warfare; and the provision of government services. 78 pages, ISBN Paper 0-89843-443-2, $12.00 per copy.

Information Technology and the New Global Economy: Tensions, Opportunities, and the Role of Public Policy (2004)
    David Bollier, rapporteur

    This report provides context and insight into the unfolding of new economic realities arising from the information revolution—how the world's players will live, learn, innovate, offer, consume, thrive, and die in the new global economic landscape. *Information Technology and the New Global Economy* draws a portrait of a changing global economy by describing new business models for the networked environment, exploring topics of innovation and specialization. Among the more creative concepts propounded at the Roundtable was an analysis of the world's economy in terms of video game theory that suggests that if developing countries are not incorporated into the world economic community in some acceptable way—if they cannot make economic progress—they could become disrupters to the entire economic or communications system. The report also explores issues of outsourcing and insourcing in the context of digital technologies moving work to the worker instead of vice versa. Participants concentrated on developments in India and China, taking note of some of the vulnerabilities in each of those countries as well as the likely impact of their rapid development on the broader global economy. 57 pages, ISBN Paper: 0-89843-427-0, $12.00 per copy.

People / Networks / Power: Communications Technologies and the New International Politics (2003)
    David Bollier, rapporteur

    This report explores the sweeping implications of information technology for national sovereignty, formal and informal diplomacy, and international politics. Bollier describes the special challenges and new rules facing governments and nongovernmental organizations in projecting their messages globally. The author further explores the relationships between the soft power of persuasion and the more traditional hard power of the military and discusses how governments will have to pay close attention to newly burgeoning social communities in order to prosper. 68 pages, ISBN Paper: 0-89843-396-7, $12.00 per copy.

The Rise of Netpolitik: How the Internet Is Changing International Politics and Diplomacy (2002)
   David Bollier, rapporteur

   How are the Internet and other digital technologies changing the conduct of world affairs? What do these changes mean for our understanding of power in international relations and how political interests are and will be pursued? *The Rise of Netpolitik* explores the sweeping implications of information technology for national sovereignty, formal and informal international diplomacy, politics, commerce, and cultural identity. The report begins with a look at how the velocity of information and the diversification of information sources are complicating international diplomacy. It further addresses geopolitical and military implications, as well as how the Internet is affecting cross-cultural and political relationships. It also emphasizes the role of storytelling in a world in which the Internet and other technologies bring our competing stories into closer proximity with each other and stories will be interpreted in different ways by different cultures. 69 pages, ISBN Paper: 0-89843-368-1, $12.00 per copy.

The Internet Time Lag: Anticipating the Long-Term Consequences of the Information Revolution (2001)
   Evan Schwartz, rapporteur

   Some of the unintended consequences of the Internet and the freedoms it symbolizes are now rushing to the fore. We now know that the network of terrorists who attacked the World Trade Center and the Pentagon made full use of communication technologies, including email, Travelocity.com, automatic teller machines (ATMs), data encryption, international money transfers, cell phones, credit cards, and the like. Is the Internet an epochal invention, a major driver of the economy for many years to come, or just a passing fad? Will the new phenomena of recent years—such as the contraction of hierarchies, instant communication, and lightning-fast times to market—last beyond the funding bubble? What is the next new economy? What are the broader social consequences of the answers to those earlier questions? This report takes a wide-ranging look at the economic, business, social, and political consequences of the Internet, as well as its ramifications for the process of globalization. 58 pages, ISBN Paper: 0-89843-331-2, $12.00 per copy.

Uncharted Territory: New Frontiers of Digital Innovation (2001)
  David Bollier, rapporteur
  This report looks critically at key insights on the new economy and its implications in light of the digital revolution. The report begins with an examination of the interplay between the current economy and the capital economy and then probes the emerging world of mobile commerce and its potential for driving the next great boom in the economy. It further explores new business models resulting from the combination of mobile communications and the new economy. 68 pages, ISBN Paper: 0-89843-307-X, 12.00 per copy.

Ecologies of Innovation: The Role of Information and Communications Technologies (2000)
  David Bollier, rapporteur
  This report explores the nature of innovation and the role of the information and communications sectors in fostering ecologies of innovation. In this context, the report examines the ways in which the creation of new ecologies is affecting significant societal institutions and policies, including foreign policies, industry and business structures, and power relationships. 44 pages, ISBN Paper: 0-89843-288-X, $12.00 per copy.

Reports can be ordered online at *www.aspeninstitute.org* or by sending an email request to *publications@aspeninstitute.org.*

The Aspen Institute
Communications and Society Program

www.aspeninstitute.org/c&s

The Communications and Society Program is an active venue for global leaders and experts to exchange new insights on the societal impact of digital technology and network communications. The Program also creates a multi-disciplinary space in the communications policy-making world where veteran and emerging decision makers can explore new concepts, find personal growth and develop new networks for the betterment of society.

The Program's projects fall into one or more of three categories: communications and media policy, digital technologies and democratic values, and network technology and social change. Ongoing activities of the Communications and Society Program include annual roundtables on journalism and society (e.g., journalism and national security), communications policy in a converged world (e.g., the future of international digital economy), the impact of advances in information technology (e.g., "when push comes to pull"), and serving the information needs of communities. For the past three years, the Program has taken a deeper look at community information needs through the work of the Knight Commission on the Information Needs of Communities in a Democracy, a project of the Aspen Institute and the John S. and James L. Knight Foundation. The Program also convenes the Aspen Institute Forum on Communications and Society, in which chief executive-level leaders of business, government and the nonprofit sector examine issues relating to the changing media and technology environment.

Most conferences utilize the signature Aspen Institute seminar format: approximately 25 leaders from a variety of disciplines and perspectives engage in roundtable dialogue, moderated with the objective of driving the agenda to specific conclusions and recommendations.

Conference reports and other materials are distributed to key poli-
cymakers and opinion leaders within the United States and around the
world. They are also available to the public at large through the World
Wide Web, www.aspeninstitute.org/c&s.

The Program's Executive Director is Charles M. Firestone, who has
served in that capacity since 1989, and has also served as Executive
Vice President of the Aspen Institute for three years. He is a communications attorney and law professor, formerly director of the UCLA
Communications Law Program, first president of the Los Angeles Board
of Telecommunications Commissioners, and an appellate attorney for
the U.S. Federal Communications Commission.